Village of Doomed Women

poems by

Thomas Patterson

Finishing Line Press
Georgetown, Kentucky

Village of Doomed Women

Copyright © 2019 by Thomas Patterson
ISBN 978-1-64662-006-7 First Edition
All rights reserved under International and Pan-American Copyright Conventions. No part of this book may be reproduced in any manner whatsoever without written permission from the publisher, except in the case of brief quotations embodied in critical articles and reviews.

ACKNOWLEDGMENTS

Some of the poems in "Village of Doomed Women" first appeared in the following journals, sometimes in slightly different form or in earlier versions:

"The Dark at the Top of the Stairs, Kiev, 1941" (*The South Carolina Review*)
"Village of Doomed Women" (*The South Carolina Review* as, "And Then")
"because she will never wear it," (*Potomac Review*)
"Still Life With Iris and Apples" (*Tiger's Eye*)
"*Romantic Dreamscapes*" (*Cider Press Review* as, "Among the Living")
"Two Lovers in *String Theory* (Time)" (*Pebble Lake Review*)
"This is What it Will be Like" (*CutBank*)
"Present & *Future* (Past)" (*Cavalier Literary Couture*)
"Leaving for Chelmno, December 8, 1941" (*Portland Review*)
"Judenfrei" (*Willard & Maple*)
"there & here" (*Crab Creek Review*)

Publisher: Leah Maines
Editor: Christen Kincaid
Cover Art and Design: Grace Augello
Author Photo: Thomas Patterson

Printed in the USA on acid-free paper.
Order online: www.finishinglinepress.com
also available on amazon.com

Author inquiries and mail orders:
Finishing Line Press
P. O. Box 1626
Georgetown, Kentucky 40324
U. S. A.

Table of Contents

Present & *Future* (Past) 1

Romantic Dreamscapes 2

The Dark at the Top of the Stairs, Kiev, 1941 3

what they didn't know about Karen, ... 4

Leaving for Chelmno, December 8, 1941 6

you're there & the white sheets are there, Roaring Spring, 1961 7

Thessaloniki, 1943 8

Stillborn, ... 9

Village of Doomed Women 10

Still Life With Iris and Apples 12

because she will never wear it, ... 13

This is What it Will Be Like 14

Judenfrei 16

Government Brochure: Instructions in Case of Military Operations Failure (2014) 17

World News Tonight, 2001 19

rip & cut 20

there & here 22

what reaching out for your hand might mean, ... 24

Two Lovers in *String Theory* (Time) 25

whoever you are, ... 26

For Margot

Present & *Future* (Past)

The dog is dreaming of his red ball
let x = the velocity of our escape
(in which you touched your neck only to discover)
in five years it will lie beneath the once tulips
from the black hole of this life this day and deep
(your throat's gone thin as a heron's throat)
in the rotting desert of dry bulbs
the Monet pastels the yellows the whites
(strands of your hair caught up in the rug)
though he won't see the hand I reach out
doomed in Darwin's scheme
(that's you bending to loosen them out)
from the emptiness the loneliness
where they will die their little deaths only the red Emperors
(like pearls of yourself wavering in the dusk)
of the room he's never been in
will dare to survive standing like guardians
(against this certain darkness)

Romantic Dreamscapes

*Is
she somewhere in
the sweet
brome meadow now the
only place
I cannot follow though in my dreams
I walk the henna meadow down, sweet felicity of
summer wind your
breath gone dry on the flush mount mirror this gurney
equipped for sleep rattles by the quickest brook that doctor
bends over forest golds and greens soft aubade in his
voice he lowers his stethoscope to the breast
of the new moon's milk he says
where beneath her mother
the bright fawn suckled in Eden's arms and the
morning stag, alarmed, ran down against his time and felt
but could not see it disappear ahead, "this line
has gone completely flat" darling
a lily too far from the sun softly
breathing folds new ones
have been made ready for this emptied space and today and
the next and the one after that I will present myself among
the living the way I should
the way I must
each day a new little
lie.*

The Dark at the Top of the Stairs, Kiev, 1941

Time was my sovereign
breathing its moments like
dying children
one following after the other
no stopping the relentless gear
of the wheel

the wheel of August when I walked
from my room to the landing window
near the stairwell

I had the gift of second sight
for two weeks I watched the children
breach the floorboards
in the hallway their peony red eyes
softening to pink
and finally going blank, flung down
gnome-like
into the limed canal
as though they were not fit to flower

my name was Danielia
I grew up in the town of Kiev
I did not go with my brother and my sister
my Imah and my Abba to the ravine at Babi Yar
I was too afraid

my red dust is sealed in the patio brick surrounding the portico
and in the spline of stone mortar where man and material
await eternity together

I was beloved of the God of twelve tribes

he alone will be my judge.

what they didn't know about Karen,

            1943

your dolls are clean and starched the boys in khaki the girls
in checks their attached pockets contain their
painted hands marked for their parts to play
the crusty hands of boys with guns
the soft and tender hands of girls in maline lace
arranged carefully near the wounded ones you saved and set aside
their skin burned with kalaazar
at Ledo, Jairampur, Burma Road,

            1960

some secrets belong to only you
milky skin dark eyes wet
flowers at her lips
dark poetry is bliss—
that was after you discovered
the newly contained finite languor of her exotic curves
and faintly blooming beneath your own skin Birth of Venus
leaving soft berries at your mouth
your throat curving downward toward your languid pale breast,

            1977

from which oncology has excised
an inexact mass abstraction with its degraded boundary
and then turned you on the tender nape
and narrow of your back and returned you
depositing you back into your room
where someone's left *The Book of Common Prayer*
for you the words stinging
like a hundred
angry bees,

1990

the ones who love you but never really knew you are waiting at your
    bedside
the room you're in insisting on an end
the morphine drip has stopped in its tracks
the useless transport tube is set aside

did you ever know a man the way a woman knows a man

they always wondered

it's remarkable how little fills some lives
they must have said to one another at the end

and yet that's not at all the way it really was,

Leaving for Chelmno, December 8, 1941

Listen to the trains with their oiled wheels come in
the hard embracing couplings steaming, clearing down
the late evening pandemonium of Lodz Station

there have always been trees blanched by winter hardness
there were always several beeches, two stricken oaks,
even one chestnut, waving its brittle arms in weakness;

there were others, stubbornly holding their last leaves,
curled green and filled with food,
soon to be blackened like all the rest;

the people's law was *listen* and when the old man spat
at the blood black night
and spoke his strange Amidah,

abreyre hob ich, and took one step
and leapt into the tunnel by the tracks,
they heard the rails ring just once

like a struck blunt bell

Die Kinder nach links!
the Kapo called
and the pallid children all lurched left
winding against the train like filigree script—

Ora pro nobis, said the girl who stood apart
then many others said, *hosanna,* or cried, *nourice*

but only two sisters whispered, *imah, imah, imah*

into each star of crescent flame.

you're there & the white sheets are there, Roaring Spring, 1961

yesterday today & tomorrow
bright, newly unsoiled

helplessly pinned to the
propped clothesline because they belong to this place & time
and no other place & time

your son
having escaped
hasn't been near this house for ten
years, inside your husband is waiting impatiently for
what by contract he believes he has the right to take
no excuses allowed don't even bother
besides, you tried that the last time and look what happened

the four corners of the yard are pushing &
pressing inward closing against you until you can
hardly breathe the daylilies are down to their final hours
like a Disney time-lapse
the stratus clouds overhead sensing entrapment in a
mid-century pastoral
stream across the sky
spinning sharp-edged engines intending to gain the future
at any cost, fleeing the
trembling
white sheets below

they have no time for the fears of womankind

so what if they must leave you behind with your hands
reaching up to your face blocking out the sun,

so nothing,

then,

Thessaloniki, 1943

The hope you lost when you began reading
these lines is covalent with the dread
I felt retrieving them
from where they lay
buried alive

the clock runs down through
our green-geared days forgiving us
its next momentum
only once when
we are young

along a boundary of clovering fields
she is not allowed the brown
breath of earth the orange tongue of the
horizon has fallen down into yet another
darkness

white lime is her shroud in this place
where she will never be discovered
the logistics of what to do with her next
became
a fait accompli

the chanted benediction of all her people
into the foothills
of Mount Chortiatis
"Je suis Juif"
 has become just another evaporating sentence

in theory it still exists
down in their tunnel in the ground
surrounding their abandoned dreams
and the melancholy geometry
of their embraces.

Stillborn,

a woman must live and die

what was my crime
birthcry cannot be

my body has
known only to a woman
a tug in a sac
against a sacred river
                        away
when something
in dreams
born—not made—
                  meadow-leaping
lark-hunting
dolly-naming
of my emptying
and because it carried
red death against

hoped-for custodian of my
opaque
of myself
i clumsily harbored
and then
because her name today
instead of her given name
i was young
believed
me,

displayed in the raiment of all her
                  failures
i will always wonder & how strange your
heard and that even I am deaf to its shrill
          music
something very wrong
28 weeks in and mandatory delivery
the clamps are like repeating rifles
are like a brutish angry man who runs

begins to go wrong
you have become the quietest space
oh my God!   is that you darling?

(*induction of labor...evacuation...*)
dearest one
womb
of all my life
the tiny neonate

memories, creator of its own
portion
streaming into a black funnel of its own
        death chamber
and then to give her a name
to have that name taken away
is stillness
decided on when
when the foolish heavens
in

Village of Doomed Women

And then in perfect silences
in loveliness
the limba tree the golden brown iroko

and the boys instructed in the rebel arts
and their childhood dead
found her where she was

and each one had his way with her
and they tied her to a wenge tree
and afterwards she didn't care anymore

by the way they left
glazy-eyed at noon
two men came at dusk

and the first man said, *tamu,*
sweet one,
because he loved her as one loves

a ruined child,
and then a death-knell of moonlight
fell on her face

not belonging
no one belonging
they knelt under Congo stars

also neatly abandoned
likewise broken instruments

and left everything there the way they found it
for some authority to find
and for God to cleanse

and then the one with him said, *basa*

and pointed to the streaked violet dark behind them
that hid the sacred stars
making it seem

that they had only been imagined.

Still Life with Iris and Apples

Crimson mouths are paling still together
another day, just like all the rest;

six white maidens, *iris laevigata*
here on the throat of the henna floor
shallow purple falls

maybe it was an accident
their tumbling from the vase like silk medallions
the vase itself dropped abruptly to the floor

it's no mystery why you left that room to come down here
anyone who's known love would have understood
at least, anyone who'd been told she was the perfect lover
once

sweet pectin pressed to the red grained wall
once intoxicating skin, bleak as a bled berry

the wounded Rome wobbled to a stop
on the same hard floor

its color is of no concern anymore
or the round, bruised eye somehow blank

sooner or later the door will open
the bright kitchen sun drawn down the funnel dust
the coffeemaker frantically beeping

the hand reaching out seems a floodlight spot

on something new, once

your neck an arcane tower
quiet
arcing
thrilling,

because she will never wear it,

because she is not wearing it, because it is not part of the
accumulation marked for the shelter, as she would
have wanted and is crinoline

even though it is blue, this dress is still a lie

tapered in here toward the waist and angled
softly out there toward the bodice
A-line pearl-like

see how he's laid it out here on their bed because
he's not prepared yet to let it go
and his hands moving down nearer the shadowy décolletage

for the last time
and transfixed by the raw abandonment of the closed-up
lock-stitch hem
he backs away from the darkness she has left behind

he is finished with lies
he will never believe another.

This is what it will be like

if you leave this house because it speaks to you night after night
asking for something back

and if there is nothing to give back
because she died

and if loneliness is a tree
dug into by an ax

or if a friend says you should give her
things away now and never look back

if you ever hope to start living again
or if the science known to your children

makes them believe they did not
expect to find anything left of her here at all

because
it is what it is

but you said, science is not art
although anyone looking from the darkness

might suspect that you've
filled the night up with an aesthetic of old ghosts

or if you invite someone over to practice
an imperative ritual

and if there is a thrilling shallow between her
shoulders tonight a tapered glassine vale
it will contain this message from you
"you have misjudged me because

by tomorrow I will have forgotten this night"
and when your lips press down against those words

in an hour of desperation
you will pretend

not to believe them.

Judenfrei
    —Berlin was declared, "Free of Jews," May 19, 1943

This is where you came in
the last of any number, type, or kind
wheeled into a *Topf Recline*
the best there was in mechanics and design

first your hair loose against your pale throat
was lit
in blues and golds
its secrets quickly furled into dust
the tunnel of your mouth fell next
breathing a hard fire with its silences
gained from the convenient room across the hall
where you slept cramped and naked
your head leaning against your mother's breast

flowering below the gates, under the crawling black, *Arbeit Macht Frei*
your torso pushed
and your narrowed hips
faltered and flaked
and their undisclosed children went with them
shoveled with your legs and feet
down and out the door;
your strongest bone
beat against the bottom brick like a block of wood
flopped off the ledge and fell into the barrel
meeting the sudden air

ahead, the summer is completed

and you have been disclosed to play your part
in the sulphur rings of orange and purple skies

in the warm breathing virgin white and green
of every guelder rose

that hungers for the earth tonight.

Government Brochure: Instructions in Case of Military Operations Failure (2014)

(The girl sitting on the curbing has just lost her mother
nevertheless, someone has put her hair up into a brave
ponytail she has her jacks in one hand her ball in the
other temporarily forgetting which to throw down first,

if a note comes to your home marked
Special Delivery—Official Business of the United States
exercise great caution in opening—the contents of the letter
are sharp as a stropped razor—
steel yourself for what you are about to read
remembering her life as a transient brightness
like the cycle of her beloved fireflies)

Dear Family of Deceased Officer,

*...only twice in our history has a M1117 ASV on recon patrol
been seen on ops with a female officer driving—*

this is a very prideful accomplishment—

(there's a place near Shinwar to secure," says an
email home, "another town defended to the nines"

The reason for the child's confusion is that her silver jacks
thrown down against the tarmac are spinning shrapnel talons
looking for a place to hook on and her rubber ball
turned red, is an enormous tire bounced against
someone's skull)

...regarding the child left behind:

*PTSD occurs in the young more frequently than one might
imagine
many suffer from this treatable yet profound
disorder—*

*Guanfacine is the safest protocol for children
with flashbacks,*

We are with you in sympathy during this difficult time,

and remain,

Military Information Services

(on any given day a grown woman will begin to say to anybody

"Sometimes, even now, I feel her hand against my cheek"

but her words will catch in her throat
like a phalanx of broken glass)

World News Tonight, 2001

In blues and golds in dusk or dark the streets
of Chowkar-Karez contain daughters mothers and
sons discovering their brothers fathers and children
each assigned a single space one on top of the other
prepared for delivery the latex holding bags flapping
in the wind the Velcro straps loosening undone

you ask for tenderness a respite a moment of solace
where it all might end—a space formed for your
mouth just to be adored to offer against all evil
two crimson sepals falling open

but those children speak to us—from where?—from
some little hell we'll read about tomorrow morning
the black type crawling across the white page
a quickly scanned hymn, *Now in the Days of Youth*,
hiding in the only invisible corner or the
downloaded *NYT* app G4 blinking to reveal infant faces

bellies heavy with warm steel
wrinkled like dried melons

if we walk darling out into this early morning rain

and if we speak exactly as if those children are our own children
in some perfect world then this interlude taken tonight
away from their suffering this act of love, ecstatic, imperative
is the prelude to
our own annihilation.

rip & cut

My sister is meeting in a tribal ritual

        this is nine years ago
when I am brought outside into an unholy space
        I am a clan family's daughter I came to America from
        Jubba River Basin because here I
        believed my womanhood might be restored
there was no place for the instruments for the practice
there
crudely dank
crushed air
intrudes like angry hands defiant of anything female joy-like
in some female's imagined future

I am nine then and I don't know what they're doing
I don't scream
my mouth is full of dry sticks

my wound is improperly healed administered
        with a rip & cut of coarse glass
        the alight tungsten above leaking
a portrait of my neutered body
into my brain

****

In her writing she has said,
        "I am proud of my mutilated body because it
        bears witness to our oppression"

and later, "I have never received pleasure in the physical
        act of love but I always seek love over and over
        for the part of it that heals"

"the souls of the tortured heal as the Siskin soothes the sky
                in passing through it
                              she is a winging
winging creature
      a soaring thing against
                an emptiness thing,"

"may my poems be my funeral
        pyre upon which my ruined body lies
        and my words
set ablaze
        sear and cleanse
                an ancient darkness"

there & here,

there, Klangazi is to Ung'aro as rose is to summer
wobbling petals beautiful beautiful child
drive on the wind
drive and then bleed into the eternal machine

all of our poems are about dying
at first when we begin them it doesn't seem that way
like the one I called "Bukavu Boys" after the two children chanting
running north from the DRC across the border to South Sudan
their small heads bobbing
leaning through grassy steeps

here,
on the silhouette of your summer lawn
two strong bones pointed from your shoulders to the tower of your neck
the down of your skin the blue of your wrist
sent out a message of contentment
you said come back
you held your hands out like two Lilies of the Nile

there, the boys emptied their AK-47's into the villagers
all of them had beautiful dark eyes the villagers had beautiful dark eyes
the boys too had beautiful dark eyes
and they finished the work they were given
and they found a spot to set themselves ablaze
and bits of them floated moonward
as though they meant nothing

here, you asked me to come back in
you said there was nothing anyone could do
no reason to run out into the night
no reason to look for the villagers
or for the boys
or for anything else left alive

coming toward you, I saw my reflection
in the landing mirror—for an instant it looked
as though I were breaking apart, my skin a kaleidoscope
of color
becoming the skin of everyone in the world at once
of my sisters my brothers
degrading into chunks
falling into the bevel at the reaches of the glass.

what reaching out for your hand might mean,

nothing is more important in this moment than
reaching out for your hand which
means I am reaching into your body
and means that I am prepared to learn everything there is to learn
to become the one you have searched for so long
the sensation of your blood into my fingertips allowing me to
become a part of the arterial maneuvering
the throb and rustle
blooming and dying
bringing color to your face and shoulders
and your slender throat
when those colors die away
it means you have entrusted me with the inside of your body
its necessity and nostalgia,

but reaching out is risky business
others inhabit you from before
and all of them will fight fiercely for every monument
they've left inside you
including a roué or two from yesteryear just
as voracious as before who will send out veinlet reminders
from their capillary encampments
trying to seduce you all over again,

this will be a fight to the death
only the one who disembarks and surrenders to the frenzied current
of what you need and who you are

will complete you,

Two Lovers in *String Theory* (Time)

They climb clouds and laugh for any meadow
("seems like 'meadow' sounds like 'waved wheat'")
These must be strings, then, with ten poles in time and space and
seems the only sky there is: kissing apples on their lips,
("feels like your arms downed and curved as glass")
devised by God who then simply let them go;
though broken rain casts earth and trees and just as bright
("but seems to be your nakedness at least")
shot through the universe which must have snapped
and light pressed back and forth always holds them near;
("just amorphous on some tender plane of grass")
curving the whole ether as they fell;
so it will always be when funneled dust still lingers
("and light, as fragile, with berries on her mouth")
so tiny they won't be missed at all

whoever you are,

it feels like forever since the days passed us by
or since i went out into the world tonight
a walking away & nothing else;
selvage from a thrown away something
a green sweater the color of sea eyes
crushed on the pavement moon behind me;
if this happens to you because someone you loved died young
don't turn and go back the way i used to do
there's nothing back there
nothing at all;

may my footsteps be shallow against every building's benighted rising—
may i become a shadow in my own diminishing—
this is how you may feel for today
and six months from today and long after that,
stepping into the past, night into morning
searching for a ghost among ghosts—

whoever you are,

how absurd the spring flowers will be

tomorrow

hearing the rest of the news

fatuously opening themselves up

hopeful

little

whisperings,

Additional Acknowledgments:

Many thanks to these friends/artists for their help in the review/or design, or who offered support/encouragement during the writing and preparation of *Village of Doomed Women*:

Carol Dube, James Cronin, Doug Ramspeck, Grace Augello, Jean Francois Allaux, (UMASS-Dartmouth, College of Visual and Performing Arts), Dedee Shattuck (Dedee Shattuck Gallery), and Colette Jonopulos (Tiger's Eye Press).

Thomas Patterson lives in Westport, Massachusetts; his poetry has appeared in 60 journals, including, *The Antioch Review, Nimrod International Journal, CutBank, New Orleans Review, The South Carolina Review,* and *Confrontation,* among many others.

He has had work nominated for the Pushcart Prize.

His poetry chapbook, *Juniata County,* was published from Finishing Line Press in May, 2017 and has been nominated for a Massachusetts Book Award.

Thomas is a graduate of Northeastern University (MA, English) and Rhode Island College (MEd, Counseling Psychology).

www.ingramcontent.com/pod-product-compliance
Lightning Source LLC
LaVergne TN
LVHW041514070426
835507LV00012B/1567